QUAILS

Complete Quails Information, The Ultimate Guide To Quails Care, Feeding, Housing, Training

Harmann Blanda

Table of Contents

CHAPTER ONE

Farming of quails

Commercial quail farming is something we'll get to in a bit, but first, what exactly is quail farming? A quail farm is a commercial operation that raises quails (or other poultry birds) for the purpose of harvesting eggs and meat for human consumption.

From what we've seen, raising quail is a simple, profitable, and fun business.

As one of the tiniest types of poultry birds, quails require very little space and attention on a farm. Japanese researchers were the first to succeed in domesticating wild quails and make their methods public.

The production of quails for commercial purposes in Japan has expanded greatly. People in many parts of the world are now raising quails for the purpose of selling their meat and eggs.

Farming quails is highly lucrative, much like raising chickens, turkeys, or ducks.

Beginning a quail farming business can be done in almost any climate. The meat and eggs of the quail are delicious and healthy.

When compared to eggs from other types of poultry, quail eggs are a superior nutritional choice. Why? Quail eggs have higher concentrations of protein, phosphorus, iron, vitamins A, B1, and B2.

In order to fulfill the need for food and nourishment, quail farming can play an important role. Quail farming is a low-cost and low-labor venture.

Qualities of Quails

• Quails are the tiniest of all birds.

The average quail weighs between 150 and 200 grams as an adult, and its egg weighs between 7 and 15 grams.

- A hen quail will lay an egg every day, without fail, once she reaches sexual maturity at around 7 weeks of age.

On average, females lay 300 eggs in their first year of life. Once that first year is over, the second year sees an increase in egg production to between 150 and 175. In subsequent years, hens lay fewer eggs than they did in their first.

In terms of nutrition, quail eggs are excellent. Compared to a chicken egg, it has 2.47 percent less fat. There is a widespread myth that consuming quail eggs can help ward off diseases like diabetes and hypertension.

Quail is a delicious and healthy alternative to other types of meat. The meat has an extremely low fat content. Therefore, quail meat is an excellent choice for those who are trying to lower their blood pressure.

Eggs come in a rainbow of colors and are aesthetically pleasing.

Quails lay their eggs in the ground and do not bother incubating them. That means you'll need a brooder or incubator to bring those eggs to life.

In a nutshell, raising quails has many benefits.

Quails are small, manageable poultry birds. The following are some of the most important reasons why you should consider opening a quail farm.

Due to their small size, quails can be successfully bred in a limited space.

Quails require less food than chickens or other poultry, so they are more cost-effective to keep.

In addition to being disease-resistant, quails have a low susceptibility rate.

The quail reaches maturity much sooner than other poultry birds.

Within 6–7 weeks of age, hens begin to lay eggs.

• The incubation period for their eggs is roughly 16-18 days.

Quail is a bird that produces meat and eggs that are both

delicious and healthy. Thus, it serves as an excellent food and dietary supplement.

• The initial investment in a quail farm is modest, and labor is inexpensive.

Quail farming is a viable commercial option. It's true that some people have jumped right into the commercial quail farming industry.

• Quails are a hardy species, experiencing fewer health issues than other birds. Thus, fewer threats exist in this industry.

Compared to other types of meat, quail meat has a lower fat content. Patients with hypertension can safely consume it.

Their ability to convert plant matter into meat or eggs is respectable. For every three kilograms of food they consume, they can produce one kilogram of meat or eggs.

Six or seven quails can be kept in the same space that a single chicken would need.

Quail eggs are cheaper than the eggs of other birds because they are smaller in size. This means that quail eggs have broad appeal and can be easily sold.

Since initial outlays are low, you can launch your company with minimal capital outlay.

Within a 0.91 square meter area, you can successfully raise 6-8 quail.

Due to the high potential for profit in commercial quail farming, many formerly employed college graduates may find new opportunities in this sector. The raising of quails is a relatively easy hobby that wouldn't interfere with your day job.

CHAPTER TWO

The Quails' Life Span

The average lifespan of a quail is between 3 and 4 years. Between 150 and 200 grams is the average weight of an adult quail. Six to seven weeks of age is when female quails begin laying eggs. Weighing 7-15 grams, each egg is medium-sized. They produce over 300 eggs every year.

The females lay gorgeous eggs. Light encourages quails to lay more eggs. Typically, they begin laying eggs in the afternoon. Their eggs have a 17-day incubation period.

A baby quail weighs about 6–7 grams when it is first born. Quail never sit on their eggs to hatch them. Keep one male quail for every five females to ensure a healthy breeding population.

It takes about two weeks for a quail chick to develop enough strength to handle the world. To successfully hatch and raise chicks, eggs should weigh between 9 and 11 grams and have a smooth, hard shell.

Beginning a Quail Farming Enterprise

Since quails are smaller than other poultry birds, starting a quail farm is a simple task. Develop a thorough strategy before launching your quail farming venture. To execute the strategy as intended.

Breeds, housing, feeding, care, and marketing should all be accounted for in a comprehensive business plan. We'll run you through the whole process in a nutshell here.

Choose the Best Races of Quail

There are currently 18 different quail species available, all of which would do well in a quail farming business. Certain breeds are well-known for their ability to lay eggs, while others are prized for their meat.

There are two main categories of quail breeds, "layers" and "broilers," that are distinguished by the eggs and meat they lay. Listed below are some of the most common types of broiler and layer quail.

Raising Layers of Quail

• Tuxedo

• Pharaoh

For the British Range, See: •
British Range

• Caucasian

Manchurian Golden

Breeding Quail for Broilers

Common Bobwhite (American)

Breasts that are white in color
(Indian)

Housing

Quail farming requires specialized housing. When constructing a home or cage for your quails, remember the advice given below.

Quail can be raised in either a litter or a caged environment. In contrast to the deep litter system, cage-based quail farming has many advantages. Cage systems have less disease and other problems, and are easier to manage.

In order to ensure that air and light can freely circulate throughout their home, they should construct a suitable ventilation system.

A cage 120 cm long, 60 cm wide, and 25 cm high is suitable for housing 50 quails.

Use wire net to create their enclosures.

- The net should be 5 mm x 5 mm in size for adult quails.

- Plastic cages are the most practical option for a quail farm's needs.

The home must be located in a safe area away from any potential danger from wild animals. You should also do everything in your power to protect yourself from potential predators.

CHAPTER THREE

Feeding

Maintaining a flock of quails requires regular feedings of a balanced diet to ensure their well-being, rapid development, and maximum productivity. The average daily diet of an adult quail is 20–25 grams of food.

Protein levels in poultry food should be 27% for chicks and 22-24% for adults. See below for a chart depicting a healthy diet for quails.

Ingredients Age

0-3 Weeks

Four to Five Weeks Old Full-Grown

Milled Wheat 48 50 50

Cake with Sesame Seeds, Numbers 23 through 22

Skate Fish 20 16 14

Wheat Bran

6 8 9

Oyster shell, broken: 2.25; 3.25; 4.25

Salt 0.50 0.50 0.50

Mineral Blend 0.25-0.25 0.25-0.25

Completeness (percentage): 100

The Making of Eggs

Having your quails in a well-lit area is essential if you want them to lay eggs regularly. Lighting and heating can be provided artificially by using electric bulbs and heaters. Use a 40-100 watt bulb for this application. Seasonal shifts can be observed in the need for heating and lighting.

One male quail should be kept with every five females if you want to have any luck hatching their eggs. Choose breeds known for their high egg production, and make sure their coop is always dry and clean to maximize your flock's egg output.

Temperature, food, water, care, and management all play a role in egg production. The right lighting is essential if you want your quails to lay the number of eggs you need. A conversation about the quail-laying lull can be seen below.

Age-Related Temperature (o Celsius)

Light (Hour) (Hour)

1 Week 35 24

2 Week 30 24

3 Week 25 12

4 Week 21-22 12

5 Week 21 12

6 Week 21 13

7 Week 21 14

8 Week 21 15

9 Week 21 16

Taking Care of Baby Quails

A quail's eggs are never incubated. Consequently, if you have access to either chickens or an incubator, you can create chicks by hatching their eggs.

The average incubation time for a quail egg is 16-18 days. In order to maximize egg production, the quail house needs to be lit for a full 16 hours every day. Raise quail chicks in a warm environment such as a brooder.

For the first two weeks after hatching, chicks need a controlled environment with artificial heat. Quail chicks develop a high level of sensitivity. Both the litter and battery system can be used to raise them successfully. The following considerations should be kept in mind while tending to quail chicks.

CHAPTER FOUR

A Comfortable Temperature

Sufficient illumination

* Adequate ventilation

• The number of quail eggs laid per square meter

Provision of Food and Hydration

Standards for sanitary upbringing

The layer quail chicks need to have their temperature and lighting adjusted accordingly. If you want to follow the below chart, you should.

Infant Body Temperature Chart (o Celsius)

Light (Hour) (Hour)

1 Week 37.7 24

2 Week 35 24

3 Week 32.2 12

Breeding

The quail is a naturally successful breeder. If you keep a healthy number of male and female quails in your farm, they will quickly breed and provide you with plenty of fertile eggs for hatching.

Diseases

When compared to other poultry birds, quails have a lower disease rate. To keep them healthy and disease-free, however, requires diligent management and attention to detail.

Successful quail farming requires expert management and attention to detail. Vaccines to prevent disease are rarely offered to them.

Quail chicks are vulnerable to extreme weather and

temperature fluctuations. So, if there is a drastic shift in the weather, they become susceptible to disease.

Take extreme caution now. The quails are severely impacted by the following diseases.

If quails contract coccidiosis, give them a solution of coaxial 20 in water (2 grams per litter) for three days. If your veterinarian has not instructed you otherwise, continue feeding this.

For Ulcerative Enteritis, feed quails a solution of 1 gram of streptomycin diluted in 1 litter of water daily for 3 days. Because of this, the disease of ulcerative enteritis will be halted.

Managed Care and Related Activities

Successful quail farming relies heavily on humane treatment of the birds.

For the most part, quails don't need as much attention as other birds because of their resilience. However, if you give the birds the attention they deserve, they will flourish and lay more eggs.

You should keep an eye on your bird's health and act quickly if you detect any changes.

Make sure your birds get their shots on time, and maintain regular contact with a local vet.

Get some of the medications you'll need in stock. You should never give your birds food or water that has been tainted by pollution.

CHAPTER FIVE

Tips for Clean and Successful Quail Farming

Follow the clean quail farming techniques described here to keep your birds healthy and laying eggs.

Maintain a dry and clean home at all times.

They should make sure that there is adequate ventilation and lighting in their home.

Separate quails of different ages to prevent aggression.

Remove sick quails from the flock and quarantine them.

The dead bird should be burned or buried.

Do not let other birds, animals, or strangers into the quail house on your farm.

• Make sure a healthy and sanitary diet is included in the feed.

Maintain a steady supply of pure water to meet their needs.

Marketing

Both quail meat and eggs are delicious and nutritional powerhouses. Thus, the demand for quail meat and other goods is well-established.

Due to the small size of quail and quail eggs, they are readily available and affordable to a wide range of consumers. That means you can focus less on product promotion.

The meat and eggs will fetch a good price at the grocery store. It is recommended, however, that you first develop a marketing plan. This is due to the fact that not every region has access to the same marketing resources.

Providing food and income for families is a top priority, and quail farming is helping to do just that.

As an added bonus, commercial quail farming can provide a viable means of supporting oneself while also complementing one's primary source of income.

Similarly, raising quails can be a lot of fun and requires little effort. Do some scouting around local farms if you're thinking about getting into this business. Just go ahead and do it.

In general, these are the measures and procedures that have proven effective for quail farms. I pray that this guide has been useful to you. May God richly bless you and your endeavors.

Myths and Realities of Raising Quails

Friends from all over the world, how are you? Ideally, life is treating you well. Over the past few days, fish farming has been a major topic of conversation. Let's take a break from talking about fish farming for a while and instead I'll explain how to raise quail. I'm hoping this piques your interest just as much as fish farming has.

I've always been captivated by the delicate grace of quails, so I started raising them some time ago. My cousin has a quail farm, and it brings me great pleasure to watch the beautiful birds she raises as they nest and produce eggs. Despite the fact that many people had cautioned me against entering the quail farming industry because of the inherent dangers involved and the fact that I didn't know anyone who could be trusted with the farm's upkeep, I was inspired by his ways and methods and decided to take the plunge anyway.

Yes, I realized then that I had made the best choice. The quails in my care are laying eggs at a rate of 95%.

Myths and legends about quails were a common topic of conversation as I traveled. Here are a few and the facts that debunk them:

When quails are exposed to pleasant sounds, they begin to lay eggs. In any case, quail will lay eggs if treated well and fed a healthy diet. It's possible that someone else is playing music that's pleasant to listen to but loud enough to drown out the sounds of passing cars and pedestrians.

As a result, quails can't play the cockfighting game. Inspiring my success in quail farming, my cousin kept cocks on his farm. He has been successful in derbies thanks to the high-quality nutrition provided by the quail eggs he feeds his cocks.

The high cholesterol and subsequent hypertension that comes from eating quail eggs is bad for our health. Everyone knows that the potassium in quail eggs helps regulate blood pressure by relaxing blood vessels and boosting circulation.

Additionally, quail eggs play a significant role in regulating blood sugar levels. Of course, it's best to eat moderately, as overeating can lead to dangerously low blood sugar.

Incubators are ineffective at hatching quail eggs. Production of both meat and eggs can be accomplished with quail farms. The latter can be fed exclusively on layer pellets, eliminating the need for a male quail or cock inside the cages. Any eggs laid by hens fed layer pellets will not hatch if placed in an incubator.

But if you want breeder quail chicks, you have to combine the females with males at a rate of one male to five females (1 male is to 5 female). Possibly you tried incubating some quail eggs you bought from the grocery store, only to discover that they would not hatch. The truth is that layer pellets were used in the production of those eggs.

Extensive cage space is needed for quail farming. The fact that the quails kept in the large cage kept flying around and became so preoccupied with their many activities that they forgot to eat convinced me that the large cages were counterproductive. In this case, standard-sized cages are all that should be provided.

CHAPTER SIX

Cage for quails that is neither too small nor too large.

The eggs of quails will never hatch because the birds refuse to incubate them. They will, in fact, eventually. A quail farmer would never wait for his birds to incubate eggs because of the time commitment involved. A better course of action would be to collect all of the eggs and place them in the incubator. Each quail builds a nest, and after laying anywhere from five to ten eggs, the hen tends to them for 16 days.

There you have it, fellas. For those of you interested in or already engaged in the quail-rearing industry, I sincerely hope that I have provided you with some motivation. I want to give my sincere congratulations to all the fish and quail farmers in the world.

There are many people who try to be experts in many different areas, but if you want to be successful in the long run, it's best to specialize.

Therefore, we decided to talk about quail farming today because it's widely regarded as one of the easiest businesses to start, and more specifically, because raising quails is one of the most enjoyable experiences a farmer can have.

To begin, let's define what quail farming isn't before we get into the more complex aspects of the industry.

When asked, "What is Quail Farming?"

In quail farming, you raise the birds for the express purpose of selling their eggs or meat on the open market, just as you might with any other type of livestock.

Since quails are the smallest poultry birds available, and since they have been domesticated through breeding, they require very little in the way of attention and care.

The Appeal of Quail Farming, Expressed.

The recent surge in popularity of quail farming is probably the most compelling argument in favor of getting into the business yourself.

In Japan, for instance, where an increasing number of people are opting for quail meat and eggs as a healthy and delicious alternative to traditional fare, this trend has become one of the most popular and lucrative in recent years.

On top of that, the process of raising quail is remarkably similar to that of raising chickens or even turkeys. They require little maintenance on your part and can thrive in a wide range of temperatures, allowing them to survive the cold season with little intervention.

Can You Get Your Vitamins and Minerals from Quail Eggs?

The nutritional value of quail eggs sets them apart from the eggs of other poultry species, but in appearance they are very similar to the eggs of other poultry species.

These eggs have a higher protein content than regular chicken eggs and are also a good source of phosphorus, vitamins A, B1, B2, and iron.

The Unique Features of Quail Farming

In the past few years, many people have decided to start farming, but they quickly realized that while they are excellent for beginners, this may be the best option for them overall.

They are easier to care for because of their smaller size and weight, and their eggs and meat fetch a higher price than those of a typical chicken. This can turn into a quick and easy source of income.

The size of quails.

Small birds are so common among them that they are designated as such in the wild (small game birds). And the fact that they're even smaller than bantam chickens is saying something.

The average quail weighs about 5 ounces, so you'll never run out of room if you keep them. Because of how little room they need, you can keep one on your porch or in a small cage. Although a coop is preferable, a cage can serve the purpose in the meantime.

It may seem like a drawback that they don't have as much

meat on their bodies as, say, a turkey or a duck, but keep in mind that the smaller the animal, the higher the price of its meat.

This means that you can expect to earn a higher price per ounce than you would for any other type of poultry bird; the exact amount will vary from region to region, but if you do the math, you'll be surprised.

This compact size is also popular among city dwellers, who can provide adequate enclosure without sacrificing too much living space.

No matter where you go, you can be sure to find plenty of "no chicken" laws, but this specifically excludes quails. Because of their small size and low maintenance needs, these birds are more often kept as pets than farmed.

Additionally, they produce a large quantity of small-sized eggs, which sell very easily and for a very profitable price, so you can easily take advantage of this if you want continuous money without the tragic butchering part.

Unfortunately, their small size also makes them simple to clean up after; however, this should not be put off unless you want your entire home to take on an unpleasant odor. They don't have a particularly strong odor, but if you're not careful, that odor can become permanently embedded in your walls.

CHAPTER SEVEN

This is a major problem for many people with any bird or pet they decide to keep as a pet. In essence, many rental units do not permit chicken because of the constant noise they make.

However, unlike most other birds, they are surprisingly quiet. Not that they never speak; rather, their conversations resemble those of a flock of wild birds rather than the morning crowing of a henhouse rooster.

The male quails, while occasionally strutting around, are generally very quiet and won't cause an interruption just because they feel like it.

Keep in mind that as you get closer they may begin making recognizable cooing and trilling noises, which can become quite loud if you're not careful. If you want to avoid a warning from the neighbors, you should avoid paying them a late night visit.

Can I Eat Quail Without Feeling Guilty?

We've gone over how typically quail are much smaller than chicken, duck, or turkey numerous times already. This means that unless you raise them by the dozens, you won't be able to harvest much meat from them. There are some quail breeds that get pretty big, but keep in mind that this doesn't necessarily make them bigger than the average chicken.

While the Bobwhite Quail is larger than the average quail and therefore more valuable to owners, you shouldn't count on it becoming a massive behemoth any time soon.

The good news is that quail reach maturity in about 18 days, so you won't have to put up with them in your apartment for too long before you can send them off to be slaughtered.

The fact that quails don't call for a lot of food to begin with is another reason they're so simple to care for. In reality, quails are simple to care for, and you can feed twice as many of them as you would a dozen regular chickens on the same amount of food. If you're looking to buy some quails, you should know that the price is typically higher than that of chicken, duck, or turkey due to the belief that quail meat is healthier.

Given that it tastes very different from regular chicken

meat, it's best to give it a try once before deciding whether or not you like it.

We are at a loss for words to describe the flavor, but can assure you that it is easily distinguishable from chicken.

To what extent do quails lay eggs daily?

Here's a tidbit that, should you ever need to deal with quails, is guaranteed to come in very handy: They lay plenty of eggs, and while their size may surprise you, you'll find that the eggs are much tastier and healthier than those from larger birds.

The average quail lays just one or two eggs per day, but given their diminutive size, you'll need a lot more of them on hand if you hope to turn a profit.

Once they reach the ripe old age of 7 weeks, they can begin laying eggs, and you can even use their eggs for your own batch.

It's funny, but as the quail industry grows, more and more people are keeping quails purely for the eggs they provide rather than for profit.

Finally, keep in mind that quails, unlike chickens, which take an average of 4.5 months before they begin laying eggs, can begin doing so as early as 2 months after birth. There is no drawback to these eggs, other than the higher price, because they can be prepared in a fraction of the time.

In terms of aesthetics, this is one of the most interesting combinations of egg colors you'll ever come across. And the best part is, each egg is completely different from the others.

Eggs are a versatile breakfast food that can be made into anything from deviled eggs to scotch eggs to pickled eggs to the traditional hard-boiled egg.

Not to mention, they are very similar to chickens in that female quails can begin laying eggs even in the absence of a male quail. This means that you can simply purchase a clutch of females and begin selling or keeping the eggs.

CHAPTER EIGHT

Just how much do quails typically set you back?

Since you've read this far, I'm going to assume that you're interested in purchasing some quails as a holiday gift for yourself. However, before proceeding, it is important to be aware of the associated costs.

However, you won't need to worry too much about going bankrupt because the average quail only costs a buck or two to purchase, depending on where you buy them.

In addition, you can get a whole batch for under $15, which is crazy low considering the potential earnings. Always aim for at least three women per make when diversifying your genders to avoid any unneeded strife.

Similarly, it can be detrimental to have too few roosters. They'll be breeding constantly, which can be taxing on your rooster. Achieving peaceful coexistence among them requires sticking to the "three by one" rule.

Uses Apart from Eggs

The feathers of quails are highly valued for their practicality in a variety of creative endeavors. Since their feathers, like their eggs, come in a wide variety of hues, the possibilities for artistic expression are virtually endless.

You can use the quails' manure as a high-quality fertilizer for whatever you're growing on the side, ensuring a more rapid and robust harvest.

In conclusion, the common quail is an excellent tool for canine education. Although it may seem cruel to fling them around an animal like a dog, they make excellent training partners.

In general, how do quails typically act?

In addition to their generally low maintenance needs, quails' sociable nature makes them among the simplest of all bird species to keep. They require little in the way of upkeep and form strong bonds with their keepers, making them quick to warm to new people.

Adult quails are extremely sensitive to handling, but young quails can benefit from occasional hand-reassuring and relocation.

Make sure you spend a lot of time with them as they get older so that they never forget that you are responsible for their well-being. The warmth of their reception will indicate whether or not you've succeeded. They are pleased to see you, and you have succeeded if they coo at you frequently.

Conclusion

In conclusion, there are many aspects of caring for quails that are similar to caring for chickens. They're pleasant company and you can have as many as a dozen of them even if you're city-dwelling.

Their small stature, along with the small and nutritional eggs and tasty meat they produce, set them apart. Although their small size makes them a poor choice for meat, they are still a popular option for beginning farmers.

They may be small, but what they lack in size they make up for in potential earnings, so keep that in mind as you peruse the store in search of a new addition for your coop.

Coturnix quail are the perfect addition to any homestead or suburban backyard. Your family can enjoy gourmet-quality quail eggs and meat with very little effort and feed.

These fantastic little birds are getting more attention due to the uptick in urban farming, but they do just as well in the country. Originating in Asia, the quail is a member of the Phasianidae family of birds, which also includes chickens, pheasants, and partridges.

The coturnix quail is a small, docile bird that can be raised in relatively cramped conditions. They reach maturity at six weeks and start laying eggs at eight weeks, making them desirable both for their meat and their eggs. The male quail's crow is not as loud or as audible as that of a rooster chicken. This makes quail a great option for city dwellers who want to start quail farming because they are friendly to their neighbors. If you're considering raising quail, as with any other livestock, you should first check with your local zoning office and the state to see if you need a special permit. Raising or releasing domestic game birds in my home state of New York is prohibited without a permit from the Department of Environmental Conservation.

Since adult Coturnix quail rarely show any interest in incubating their young, most of today's quail chicks spend their first few weeks of life in one. Chicks hatching from quail eggs after 17-18 days of incubation are about the size of your thumb.

Though slow at first, the chicks pick up speed quickly after they start eating finely crushed game bird feed and drinking water a couple of hours after hatching. They really do seem to enjoy dying and are quite capable of drowning in a quail waterer. Therefore, we provide the birds with a few waterers made from recycled soda bottle caps. To keep them from disappearing into the hole, we put a marble in the middle.

The first few weeks of a quail's life, just like a chicken's, are spent under a heat lamp. Accidental exposure to cold can be fatal in a very short time frame. Upon reaching adulthood, the birds reach a height of about five inches and a weight of 3.5 to 5.5 ounces. There appears to be a 1.5- to 4-year lifespan distribution.

As adults, Coturnix quail only need the bare minimum to stay healthy. Provide them with a warm, dry place to live, some fresh water, and some high-protein game feed, and you've got everything they need to flourish.

Growing quail in welded wire cages that resemble rabbit hutches is the preferred method of most quail farmers. To prevent injury to the birds' feet, the wire used to make the floor should have openings no more than 1/4 inch in diameter. Additionally, wire aids in preventing the eggs and birds from getting dirty. Only one male should be kept in each section of the cage. If there is another male in the cage, they will fight to the death over who gets to be the alpha male and who gets to be the hens' servant. Less daylight hours in the winter will limit laying activities unless additional lighting is provided. Quail hens can only lay eggs if they get 14 hours of sunlight each day. Water bottles designed for rabbits are a better option than the quail waterers sold in most pet stores. The birds won't be able to foul the water, and they only need to be refilled every few days, so there aren't many daily chores involved in quail farming.

However, despite their docile nature, quail have a tendency to be flighty. In the event of an escape, they can be difficult to catch with a net. We learned the hard way how challenging it is to capture one of these creatures. Their bodies are the perfect size for squeezing through narrow openings. They will most likely never come back once they have escaped.

The Texas A&M is the most well-liked species of quail in the United States for use as meat. They reach a weight of 10–13 ounces in just seven weeks, which is significantly faster than the average for Coturnix quail.

When raised in the right conditions and with the help of artificial lighting, a Coturnix Quail hen can produce 200 to 300 eggs in a single year.

Perhaps you're thinking that you don't need quail on your farm since chickens can serve the same purpose. The time it takes to see a profit from chicken farming is much shorter than that of quail farming. When a hen reaches sexual maturity, which occurs between 18 and 26 weeks of age, she will start laying eggs. In the same time frame, a single quail hen can produce anywhere from 72 to 120 eggs. One hen has a realistic chance of laying 36 eggs, of which you can eat at least some of them, and hatching about 25 new quail chicks, with which you can begin the process all over again. Of course, roughly half of those 25 chicks will be male and therefore incapable of reproducing naturally. But that's okay, because at 7 weeks old, they make a delicious grilled meal.

After deciding to raise quail, you'll need a plan to keep your birds healthy and productive. No need to overcomplicate things here. You might not need to do any further preparation if your household already has plans to consume the meat and eggs. It is important to research the local market if you want to sell your birds or eggs there.

A quail farm can expand into several different markets. Because of their versatility, quail eggs have gained widespread acclaim in the Asian culinary community. Perhaps you should target the Asian market if you live in a region where the Asian population is expanding. Even better... look for an Asian market that will sell your products.

Live quail are a popular choice for some hunters and dog trainers when working with their canine companions. If you have a lot of older, unproductive birds, this might be the answer. Start with the local game hunting clubs for information. Some game farms even go so far as to buy birds specifically to stock their shooting ranges with.

People looking to buy either hatching eggs or live birds might respond to an ad posted on Craigslist. Depending on the regulations surrounding animal slaughter in your region, there may also be a need for fully dressed birds. People who try quail meat for the first time will be hooked.

The average hatching time for quail is 21-25 days, but only 16-17 days for Coturnix quail. It is important to take special precautions when setting up watering containers for quail chicks, as they are susceptible to drowning in ordinary containers. Carolyn's family has a tradition of using the caps from soda bottles, with a marble placed in the center, to prevent children from drowning.

Boiling quail eggs makes for a nutritious snack for toddlers and preschoolers who enjoy eating finger foods. They're perfect for packing in a lunch because they're easy to peel after being cooked in boiling water with a splash of white vinegar.

Quail eggs are in high demand by caterers for making deviled eggs, especially if you live in or near a major city. Eggs served in bite size portions are the epitome of a hip party appetizer. You can charge more at upscale supermarkets for your farm-fresh eggs.

Keeping your bevy (the proper name for a group of quail) at the optimal size to avoid feeding unnecessary birds is simple once you have established the business strategy for quail farming. If there is a drop in the demand for eggs and meat, the surplus can be slaughtered and frozen for later use. Fertile eggs can be stored until the demand for eggs increases again. In only eight weeks, we have a full complement of eggs and meat again.

Quail farming is easy to start up and maintain with minimal effort, high-quality feed, and delicious recipes.

CHAPTER NINE

Quail with a mushroom stuffing

Four full-grown quails have been skinned and weighed.

Two Tablespoons of Extra Virgin Olive Oil

1 minced garlic clove

Two diced onions

Approximately 2 cups of sliced fresh moonlight mushrooms

1 pound of bread, cut into 2-inch cubes

Chopped thyme equivalent to 2 tablespoons

2 tablespoons of chopped rosemary

Approximately 2 tablespoons of chopped parsley

Spice it up with some freshly cracked black pepper and kosher salt

1/4 cup of salted butter, softened

Directions:

To bake successfully, preheating the oven to 350 degrees Fahrenheit (175 degrees Celsius) is required. The quail should be deboned from the back, but otherwise left whole.

Olive oil and minced garlic should be heated together in a large frying pan over medium heat. Throw in an onion, and cook it down until it's brown and caramelized. Prepare the mushrooms by adding the slices and cooking for 1 minute. Take the pan off the stove immediately.

Incorporate the bread crumbs and the chopped herbs. Put

some salt and pepper on it, and season to your liking.

Fill the cavities of the birds with the stuffing mixture, dividing it evenly. Get the birds back to their original size and shape, then wrap them in foil and brush them with melted butter. Prepare a 15-minute roasting time in the oven for the quail. Cook for another 7 minutes with the foil open. Take it out of the oven and serve it on a bed of rice. Enjoy!

THE END

www.ingramcontent.com/pod-product-compliance
Lightning Source LLC
Chambersburg PA
CBHW061058250726
48653CB00001B/456